Mission Statement

To add to the education and understanding
of rebound benefits to health and learning

Copyright © Sheila Steele
B.Ed, C.L., C.R.*
*(Bachelor of Education, Certified Lymphologist, Certified Reboundologist)

ISBN 1-4392-0025-4
Certificate of Registration Txu1-167-382
"Moving to Learning –Bouncing Gross Motor Lab"

To order additional copies, please contact us
BookSurge Publishing
www.booksurge.com | 1-866-308-6235 | orders@booksurge.com

Disclaimer: This manual is not intended as a substitute for prescribed
therapies of physicians or therapists, and no information in this manual is
meant to be taken as medical advice, diagnosis or recommendation for
treatment of any disorder.

Contents

Author's Preface

Many people have heard there are alternative or supplemental approaches to improving brain and body function that DON'T involve drugs. I'm here to testify of specific use of a mini-trampoline, or 'rebounder'. This manual explains how the simple NON-INVASIVE bouncing on a quality rebounder can unclog sluggish lymph and stimulate neural pathways to do these things: improve physical health, calm stress, help think better and improve balance and memory FOR ALL AGES!

It is hoped that by reading and using the protocol suggested, dollars will be saved, people will actually function better and the word will spread. This is a manual for grandparents, parents, home-schoolers, teachers and therapists who seek a supplemental or alternative approach!

We all see the societal changes that we live in an ever increasing sedentary society where many kids are driven everywhere (for safety as well as convenience), spend too much time in front of the television or computer, eat too much junk food and generally operate at less than their potential. The result is a sluggish metabolism and more susceptibility to infection and disease. Not only that, behavioral symptoms such as defiance, slouching, being easily distracted and withdrawn, rubbing or scratching....etc.....are strong indicators that these symptoms indicate a lack of sensory-motor maturity needed to succeed--especially in school-- according to many experts in the field of learning (see 'credits')

Let me explain briefly: When the body doesn't work right due to circulatory stagnation, the transmission of information to and from the brain is likewise sluggish or dysfunctional. Science has confirmed that regular exercise benefits both the mind and the body. Neuropeptides (hormones) release the body's own morphine; we've heard of the endorphin 'high'. Well, keeping this 'happy high' occurs when our immune system stays healthy through rebound exercise which flushes out toxins that cause disease, and we feel great!

As a learning therapist, certified reboundologist, lymphologist and school teacher, I have used and trained others in rebounding since 1995 in Canada, the U.S. and South Africa. We are in a new age of 'bioenergetics' which links dysfunctions in health or mental problems to our body's electrical system. Bouncing, as you will discover, done with an intentional protocol, is a means to maintaining, and even reversing, disruptions in the body-brain electrical system. We can reduce learning dysfunction to improve academic success and re-energize our bodies against the ravages of ageing through rebounding! My mantra for years has been:

Learning to Move is Moving to Learn

So, breeze through the formalities and technicalities in Part One. Part Two describes the childlike fun way to use the rebounder, which I designed while in Africa.

I offer workshops to demonstrate aspects of this manual, so please contact the publisher or me directly at the email at end of book. A second manual "Come to Your Senses" is offered to workshop attendees which adds another component in my 'Balance & Bounce Lab' by additional use of a balance board.

What is a rebounder?

The equipment used, the 'Rebounder', is best known to the layman as a 'mini-trampoline'. It is also referred to an 'energizer', 'bouncer' or 'lymphasizer'. Some of the general public may think the 'mini-trampoline' is like the large unit used for stunts, that is why the term 'rebounder' is preferred to distinguish the rebounder's specific utility for health and learning enhancement. The quality unit I use is Needak rebounder. (I am a distributor: details at end of this manual)

Tigger Tail Bounce

Next, we have to know how the rebounder is used to improve brain/body coordination: Sensory Integration.

What is SENSORY INTEGRATION?

Sensory integration refers to the important function of synchronizing the electrical impulses between brain and body parts, so that when you get a signal or stimulus visually, aurally or by touch, the neurotransmitters which send and receive messages to and from the brain work properly. Like riding a bike, all the senses are integrated to respond automatically.

Often we develop **traffic jams** (clogging) in our circuitry transport system that need jiggling loose. How? By rebounding, of course!

Lets get excited about rebounding !

Almost anyone can have the health benefits, even the blind, those in wheel chairs, mentally or physically handicapped.

It can calm babies down

It can help students think more clearly and learn better

It can help with balance and memory in old age

PHYSICAL & EDUCATIONAL BENEFITS
of bouncing on the Rebounder

1. Improves <u>STRENGTH</u> and <u>TONE</u> of all cells in the body, including bone, muscle and skin.

2. Improves efficiency in REMOVING TOXINS from the body, thus contributing to better physical health and immunity to disease.

3. Improves VISUAL perception: 80% of learning comes through the eye. By doing the focusing exercises while bouncing, undetected field vision, near point or muscle action dysfunctions are addressed.

4. Contributes to ACADEMIC success by clearing neural blockages to readiness for learning.

5. Improves MEMORY with rhythmic timing at the bottom of the bounce (see Education Benefits & vision)

6. Decreases Attention Deficit and Dyslexia

7. Improves BALANCE, coordination, & sense of timing through constant rhythmic movements.

8. Improves SELF-ESTEEM: this is such fun; smiles accompany success.

9. Sets the Vestibular-Ocular Reflex (VOR) in motion for reading. If this important reflex is not working, reading is not possible (see the CopyCat Chart)

10. Convenient! This can be done at home; requires little space and is an efficient use of time.

There is a PHYSICAL benefit to bouncing! Dr. Sam West calls it 'lymphasizing'. Bouncing on the rebounder creates a necessary pressure around our healthy cells to <u>push out trapped toxins</u> into the lymph system where they can then be released. The 'lymphasizing' technique is not only fun, but it keeps our circulation going by the muscular movement and deep breathing when trained properly. This is further described under Lymphatic-Emphatic Choo-choo breathing section in this manual. (See Dr. West's book, "The Golden Seven Plus One")

We have to face the fact that we live in an ever increasing sedentary society where many kids are driven everywhere (for safety as well as convenience), spend too much time in front of the television or computer, eat too much junk food and generally operate at less than their potential. The result is a sluggish metabolism and more susceptibility to infection and disease.

Circulatory Stagnation:
Sedentary lifestyle of too much sitting & not enough exercise; Junk food and a lowered immunity to disease. FLUSH IT OUT!! REBOUND! FEEL GREAT!

When the body doesn't work right due to this circulatory stagnation, the transmission of information to and from the brain is likewise sluggish or dysfunctional. Science has confirmed that regular exercise benefits both the mind and the body. Neuropeptides (hormones) release the body's own morphine; we've heard of the endorphin 'high'. Well, need I say more?

To acquire these benefits, my specifically designed 'Gross Motor Lab' works best. Such involves using large muscle groups in conjunction with sensory stimulation – visual, auditory, kinesthetic. To accomplish this, I've used the theme "MOVING TO LEARN" with the more specific description as 'BODY BOUNCING' on a quality rebound unit (more on this at end of manual).

Let's begin with an understanding of how rebounding works to improve the brain and body function: It needs to be explained in terms of the LYMPHATIC SYSTEM.

WHEN THE LYMPH ISN'T MOVING, THE BRAIN & BODY GET SICK – NOT FUNCTIONING WELL. The best way to move toxifying lymph is through REBOUNDING.

What is the LYMPH system?

The lymphatic system is an accessory route which carries large particles (dead cells/toxins) away from the interstitial spaces around cells, which could not otherwise be removed by absorption directly into blood capillaries. This is an essential function, otherwise we are heading towards a deathly demise, says Dr. West , The Golden Seven Plus One – Conquer Disease (Samuel Publishing Co., UT, 1981)

Lymph is the clear water and dissolved nutrients that come after having passed through capillary walls. We have 12 quarts of lymph versus 3 quarts of blood plasma in our bodies – so we should know something about it! The lymphatic system is not connected to the heart circulatory system, but is a series of one-way valves that 'suck' like a vacuum and dump into the subclavian vein where clear lymph is returned to the blood stream and the toxins sent to the excretory organs. (Further investigation can be made through Dr. West's book)

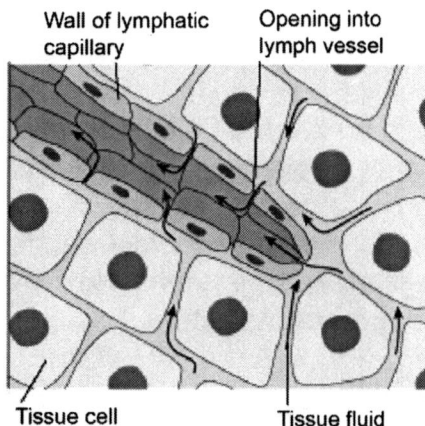

Wall of lymphatic capillary   Opening into lymph vessel

Tissue cell   Tissue fluid

The <u>LYMPHATIC SYSTEM</u> has been called the...

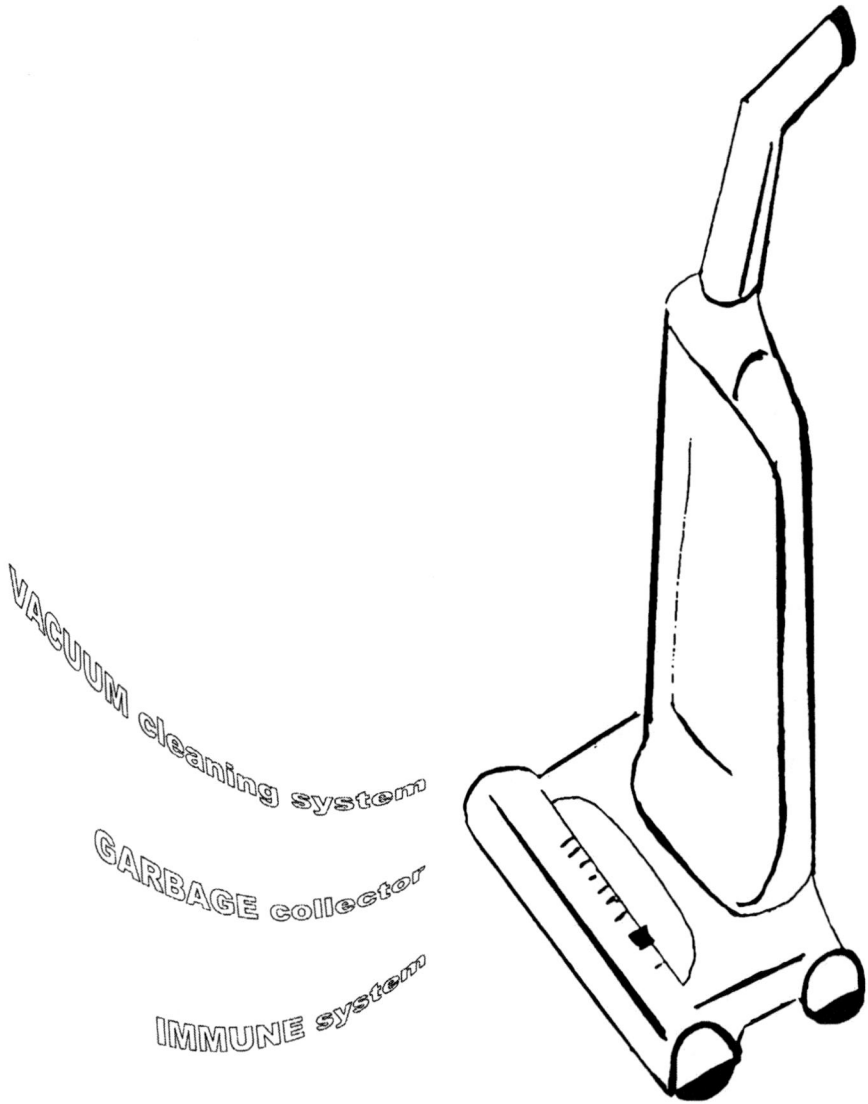

VACUUM cleaning system

GARBAGE collector

IMMUNE system

<u>LYMPH</u> fluid circulates within a system of tubes, having one way valves. **<u>The lymph fluid is circulated only through movement</u>**, which varies the pressure on the system. So, sitting doing nothing causes stagnation and illness! The lymph 'vacuums' the toxins, dead cells, and other debris away from the body's cells, releasing these through excretory system. Now, oxygen and glucose can feed cells and the whole body functions better!

Is this starting to make sense?

Because jumping vertically on the unit involves the forces of <u>deceleration</u>, <u>acceleration</u> and <u>gravity</u>, it stimulates EVERY CELL in the body, at the same time--internal organs, skin, muscles – everything!

At least 30 chemicals in the cerebral spinal fluid which bathe the brain are circulating more actively with rebound activity.

At the bottom of the bounce, each brain cell is stimulated, making this the <u>critical point</u> of learning.

Memory is enhanced in this alpha wave state at the bottom of the bounce. The brain is very programmable at this point. Times tables, spelling words or facts rehearsed will be fixed in memory. You will read further on this under Educational Benefits & Vision.

Because there is no involuntary circulatory pump in the lymphatic system, (like the heart) <u>the only way the debris moves is when YOU move</u>. And, the more efficiently you move, the healthier and 'brighter brained' you will be. NASA studies have shown that rebounding is at least 68% more efficient that other joint-jarring exercise for lymphatic effect (see needak-rebounders.com for complete report),

Because of this lack of a pump, this is how rebounding works to cleanse your system:

Increased pressure at the BOTTOM of the bounce CLOSES valves and fluid STOPS.

At the TOP of the bounce (anti-gravity off the mat) pressure decreases, valves OPEN and fluid FLOWS.

MOVING TO LEARN –

The **BOTTOM** of the BOUNCE

At the bottom of the bounce EVERY cell is stimulated by the combination of 3 forces: **acceleration, deceleration and gravity**.

At the bottom of the bounce, body weight increases two times normal (2G's). You can demonstrate this effect by bouncing lightly on your bathroom weigh scale as you see the needle increase to a higher weight. At the top of the bounce, when you are suspended in air, you are weightless.

Thus cells are mechanically stimulated by the bouncing which sets off a chain reaction to **chemically**, **electrically** and **neurologically** alter cells. The lymphatic system is especially affected as the removal of toxins that cause illness, plus sluggish circulation, is activated by the bouncing. The cells chemically convert the nutrients to electrical energy so we can function. The neurotransmitters, now highly activated through the stimulation are **alert** to send messages to and from the brain.

The <u>bottom of the bounce</u> is the point of learning:

REPETITION for MEMORIZATION
is a PRE-REQUISITE to learning
therefore....

Rebounding Activities improve memory
because bouncing stimulates cells

neurologically

electrically

chemically

mechanically

10

Bottom of the Bounce

is the POINT of LEARNING

G-Force Rebounding activites stimulate every cell
REPETITION Reinforces Memory Storage & Retrieval

3 forces combine to stimulate every cell:

ACCELERATION

DECELERATION

GRAVITY

Bottom of the bounce: 2G's force where cellular engines are revved! Toxins cleared out, nutrients converted to electrical energy, and neurotransmitters 'charged' to send messages between body and brain.

Repetition of the G-force and the learning demand (visual charts or auditory chants) which is reinforced at each bounce, indelibly records the new learning, if using the suggested protocol. For example, when a child recites times tables or spells words the bottom of the bounce, <u>the rhythmic movement and multisensory repetition moves learning from short-term to long term memory for later retrieval</u>. (Aha! Yes, this is sensory-integration, synchronization, automaticity!)

MOVEMENT is EDUCATION..... what protocols are best?

Moving to Learn is Learning to Move

The balance, coordination, and rhythmic timing are manifestations of internal cellular education.

So, watching people bounce awkwardly while attempting recitation of alphabet or numbers shows their cells have NOT been educated.

All cells think, all cells store memory, but they have to be taught. Think of the precision of a pianist whose brain and body memorize exact finger placement, modulation and sequence to be played.

Cheetah Chase

VISION & REBOUNDING

Would you believe that four out of 10 school children are visually handicapped?(source: College of Optomitrists, 1997) If schools only test for 20/20 vision, they are only testing visual acuity ad sharpness seen at 20 feet, but miss detecting 75% of children who have visual perception problems such as: field of vision, near point and muscle action.

VISION IS A PERCEPTION PROBLEM OF THE BRAIN. **IF THE VISUAL STIMULUS GETS GARBLED IN THE PROCESSING ACTION OF THE BRAIN, THEN IT IS STORED IN MEMORY <u>AS THAT DEFECTIVE IMAGE</u>.** For example: Unless the child's brain processing is corrected, the child will always see trees with no distinct leaves—if that was the way the perception was first stored. Visual processing such as this becomes more invisible and complicated to detect.

<u>Does the eye see the leaves on a tree</u>?
If vision is dysfunctional, then whatever was first seen is processed and stored, and believed to be 'true'

VISUAL PERCEPTION IS A LEARNED BEHAVIOR — just as walking or talking! The difference is that the child <u>cannot see through your eyes</u> to mimic visual perception as he can in walking and talking.

A child learns visually by:

<u>SPATIAL AWARENESS</u>: Identifying where s/he is...How do my arms move when I throw? When I eat? How much energy do I need to hit that target? How do I balance on the bike? Controlling direction and movement is assessed according to gravitational force. **So, basic to learning is the subconscious awareness of gravity's influence on movement.** This awareness is learned through coordinating movements with the bottom of the bounce

<u>COORDINATING LEFT and RIGHT</u> halves of body. In vision, the eye muscles of both eyes must focus together the same distance and direction to correctly pick up the message. In walking, to become automatic, the body learns to adapt skeletal and muscular movement to gravity in a sensory-motor coordinated sequence of movements. Gross Motor Lab activities such as the rebounder focusing activities address this.

MEMORIZATION associating self with object size, shape, depth, speeds, locations, distances. Use of chants with specific movements requires on-cue awareness. Other activities such as bouncing a ball or beanbag on the rebound mat also requires brain-body recall and adjustment to object.

VISION IS LEARNED BEHAVIOR
80% of all we learn comes through the eye

VISUAL PERCEPTION MUST BE INTEGRATED
with our other senses for maximum benefit

"The trampoline (rebounder) contributes more to the organization of visual perception than any other known device" (Dr. G. N. Gettman, O.D., in Miracles of Rebound Exercise by Albert E. Carter, 1979)

"Clinical and research studies indicate that the trampoline (rebounder) can provide experiences that influence a child's academic success" (Dr. G. N. Gettman, O.D., in Miracles of Rebound Exercise by Albert E. Carter, 1979)

"Gravity is the common denominator of all exercise; the greater the gravitational influence on the body, the stronger each muscle will become when overcoming that opposition." (A.E. Carter's Miracles of Rebound Exercise)

Many authorities recognize that READINESS for new learning is DEPENDENT on freedom, comfort and control of movement, as indicated above.

This information has been around over 40 years, but it is still not fully appreciated. Research at the Gesell Institute of Health, the Optometric Center of New York, the Texas Association of Learning Disabilities, and Structure of Intellect of Oregon plus many individual doctors and educators knew in the late 1970's that <u>movement exercise was associated with learning success, and that problems begin when an incoming message is processed incorrectly in the brain.</u>

More research since then has proven too many that vision can be improved with exercise (resources at end). The use of the term 'sensory integration' includes five senses for learning: visual, auditory, kinesthetic, tactile and vestibular – all related to the GROUNDING, or working with gravity.

CAN REBOUNDING AFFECT BEHAVIOR and LEARNING DYSFUNCTION?

Has it ever occurred to you that kids who are behavior problems might not know HOW to learn in a classroom situation? KIDS CANNOT PROCESS INFORMATION PROPERLY UNLESS 'GROUNDED', therefore their bad behavior is a manifestation of lack of control; and **many become relegated to 'special needs' classes as they are thought to be learning disabled. Possibly a mistake!**

According to Dr. G.N. Gettman (1993) in use of the mini-trampoline for short-term memory and sequencing, stated that" difficulties with learning can lead to a range of negative consequences…. – to emotional instability, depression and social isolation." So, it's in the community's best interest to become acquainted with resources such as this and not dismiss it! (See p.3 of Learning Connection Program in Queensland Schools, Sept. 2000)

With some simple and fun exercises on sensory motor equipment like the rebounder to coordinate and 'ground' the mind and body, there would be greater self-esteem and less behavior problems.

> **Grounding is knowing where your body is in space; and focusing inward, also called 'centering'.**

Kids don't consistently get letters and numbers backward and mixed up if they are grounded. This specifically has to do with laterality, or knowing right from left sides. This is a <u>fundamental</u> pre-requisite the brain must have for higher levels of learning.

For example, Dr. Sam West reports in his book <u>The Golden Seven Plus One</u>, that Special Education children respond to 'lymphasizing' --rebound bouncing. He cites an example of a teacher in California who tested the theory of improving health and learning. She had children from ages 8-11 with poor coordination and learning dysfunctions. "For the first three months, their coordination was so bad they couldn't stand on the lymphasizer without assistance. Somewhat amazingly, these children who could not previously speak or write their name could do so by the end of two terms. (op.cit. p.149)

In my work in South Africa, the success was quite evident. Students and teachers remarked about the bounce activities as to how they loved the terms such as "teeter-totter toes" and doing 'chicken', 'kangaroo' and 'cheetah' movements. Bouncing addressed their need to be active in a fun way, reduced the wiggles, and helped them be more attentive during academic learning. (Gauteng Province, S.A. 1997).

15

Another word on GROUNDING

'GROUNDING' THROUGH MASSAGING 'GAIT POINTS'

The gait points are located between the joints of the toes, top and bottom, and on the side joints. We massage them through "Froggie Feet" exercise (described in Part Two). Massaging the gait points helps us to ground our energies.

If gait points are 'switched off', it can result in over-tiredness, irritability, lack of concentration, being cold all the time, or problems with sleep, balance and back problems. One way you switch off your grounding by wearing cramped shoes and synthetic socks.

While some of the children are sitting waiting to have their turns, have them 'squeeze between their toes, setting a foundation for greater success of the rebound activity.

And as adults, before putting on those sports shoes, massage the gait points! Another suggestion is: even before you get out of bed, sit up and just quickly massage between the joints of your toes. Smile, too. Set a good tone for the day!

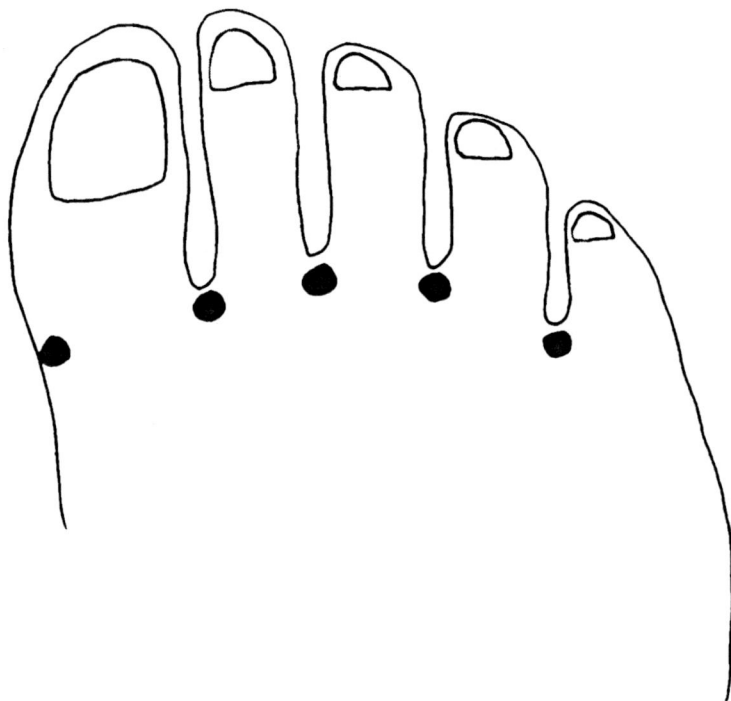

ELECTRIC FEET!

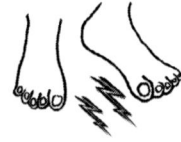

Facts for your greater understanding of the benefits of the Rebounder

- Electrical energy is produced by our cells. The body works electrically! For example:

    1. Food we eat is converted chemically into electricity so we can function.

    2. Thought waves are electrical.

    3. Energy from the eyes is electrical.

    4. Muscles work by electrical impulses from the brain.

- Proper functioning of our nervous system depends on efficient transfer of impulses from one neuron to another (synaptic gaps). 'Efficient' is the key word. Recall the term 'grounding'? Balancing the body/brain coordination of electrical stimulus-response signals is grounding.

- With the use of rebounding equipment, proper electrical conduction between the two brain hemispheres is stimulated. That means that dyslexics and A.D.H.D.-- who usually have one side of the brain working faster than the other--will become 'balanced' and able to think and move with greater ease.

- Also, did you know...

Muscles store repressed psychological inhibitions and tensions which are released through use of sensory motor equipment (such as the balance board and rebounder). Many unknown emotional factors contribute to stress while learning! Electrical transmission between body/brain while doing these exercises can facilitate release of 'toxic' emotions. Wow! Keep this in mind!

Note: If you feel a little woozy or tingling while toxins and acid deposits are being released and the body restores natural balance, just step off the rebounder, walk around and retry. Remember, this is good! When you get on again, do it for less time than you did before, letting your body adjust.

Stocking or bare feet contacting the mat while bouncing best helps trigger the electric energy reflexes in the feet.

Lymphatic - Emphatic
CHOO-CHOO BREATHING

There is a breathing rhythm (slow, slow, quick-quick-quick) that seems to enhance learning as well as promote general health. Dr. Sam West's program of lymphatic breathing clears out toxins while walking or exercising on the 'LYMPHASIZER' (rebounder). He states that unless we engage in deep breathing we will have toxins in our body no matter whatever else we do! And, as learned earlier, toxins clog the transmission of signals to the brain, which interferes with learning!

Dr. West's 'choo-choo sounding breathing rhythm must be some universal rhythm, because I, too, have used this for years in teaching vowels: "a, e, i-o-u" (slow, slow, quick-quick-quick). I employ it when rehearsing phonics with my students, on the rebounder. For instance, I hold up a picture card with the letter sound such as the short sound for 'a' as in 'apple' and they chant "a, a, a-a- apple" as they bounce rhythmically. Thus, they combine the effects of lymphatic rhythmic breathing with learning! Note that while on the rebounder, the <u>pace</u> of the jumping stays the same:

1	2		3&	4&	(pacing is 4 jumps)
'a'	'a'		'a-	a- apple'	

Rehearse while walking or clapping, using the 'choo'-choo rhythm. You can say "sh-sh" instead of 'choo-choo', (it still sounds like a train). Be **'emphatic' lymphatic** as you exhale forcefully in this rhythm:

Sh-Sh   Sh-sh-sh (slow, slow, quick-quick-quick)

This is wonderfully energizing!! Children as young as two have done it. Also, it adds an auditory support to your 'lymphasizing'. That is, it keeps you in rhythm and on task. Soldiers in marches always have a drummer of some song to keep them in pace. You can discover this yourself by moving to music, then turning off the rhythmic stimulus and try to keep the same enthusiasm and pace – You will find you are less energized and motivated.

SUMMARY POINTS:

HOW and WHAT does REBOUNDING do for the learning disabled?

Rebounding learning therapy synchronizes electrical impulses, makes movement automatic, reduces stress and coordinates the right and left sides of the body. All of this is called 'sensory integration" where the senses of vision, touch, hearing, and skeletal-muscular are working together. Sometimes there is a neurological short-circuit in the transfer of messages between muscles and the brain. Once electrical impulses are flowing freely, then communication between brain and body is easy and relaxed.

So, being 'learning disabled' means there is a short-circuit as the cause. You may be uncoordinated, lose your place while reading, be hyperactive, or slow at performing tasks. You are 'out of sync' or out of balance. Rebounding is used to speed up learning and help slow learners, often with behavior problems, to maintain self-esteem, and improve school performance

My method of using rhythmic chants (see the Animal Moves in Part Two) **integrates** the visual, auditory and kinesthetic senses to maximize learning and memory. Think of the nursery rhyme chants you learned as a child that still stick with you! They have a cadence and rhythm that is built into your memory.

Happy Hippopotamus

NUTRITION!!

Thank goodness some people are waking up to the dangers of soft drinks and those energy drinks, but there is more attention to whole foods diet required. The following is an educational summary of some needed facts:

MINERALS: sadly neglected. Soil contains less, and we lose food value through importation and genetic experimentation. Minerals also need vitamins to work together properly. The following minerals enhance brain function, so become aware of choosing a good product:

- CALCIUM (the King mineral): very important for function of all cells, especially nerve transmission and muscle activity through electrical/chemical pathways. Calcium is found in every cell and enzyme system!

- ZINC: without it, there is reduced visual memory and impaired cognitive development.

- IODINE: needed by the thyroid hormones for comprehension

- IRON: boys and girls going through puberty need this important mineral when the body experiences hormonal stress, otherwise suffering poor resistance to disease, fatigue, and dizziness. Elderly people need it too, for improving brain activity.

VITAMINS: All are important, but need to be taken with minerals. The vitamins especially relevant to brain function are:

- A,C,E: The 'antioxidants' which boost the immune system, protect the heart and arteries.

- B: the stress vitamin. A good B vitamin complex helps form the myelin sheath wrapped around nerve cells which aids in the transmission of messages from brain to body, and is important for normal growth. Without Vitamin B, there are mood changes, irritability, headaches, sugar cravings, insomnia. Make sure the product also has 100% RDA for Biotin and Folic Acid.

WATER, WATER, WATER! We are 70% water (5% blood, 15% intracellular fluid, 50% inside the cells). We lose 10 cups per day just in normal activity. This amount must be replaced daily to be in balance. You get water from fruits and some foods, so that counts. A drink of water before academic 'thinking' activity reduces stress within four seconds—it begins to oxygenate the blood which gives it to the cells.

- LECITHIN (phosphatidyl choline) transforms in the body to aceylcholine— vital for nerve message transmission! It unclogs fat in the liver and cholesterol in the arteries. Fat and oil are necessary in the body. With lecithin, these molecules can hold both oil and water, keeping them inn solution so that they are unable tos ettle out and form dangerous deposits. For the brain, each time you take lecithin, chemicals essential for signal transmission are produced.

- FLAX SEED OIL: found to improve behavior of both schizophrenics and juvenile delinquents when other resources such as counseling have failed! (Energy Time: Jan/98)

HERBS:
- GOTA KOLA: oriental herb to enhance memory and brain function

- GINKO BILOBA: found to improve memory (especially in Alzheimer patients)

PART TWO

Practical Rebounder Exercises

Knees Drop Now!

HOW TO TEACH AND USE THE REBOUNDER – BABIES:

1. "CUDDLE BLANKET" - STRADDLING: Lay child on rebounder mat (use blanket underneath for comfort), and stand on rebounder, straddling child, holding edges of blanket so that you can rock child gently and safely as you bounce. Recite any favorite nursery rhyme while you do so. Example:

> *"Momma's Little Baby loves short'ning, short'nIng,*
> *Momma's little Baby loves Short'ning Bread"*

or

> *"Sing a Song of Sixpence, Pocket full of rye,*
> *four and twenty blackbirds baked in a pie.*
> *When the pie was open, the birds began to sing,*
> *wasn't that a dainty dish to set before the king"*

and so on...

1. "CUDDLE HUDDLE" - SITTING: on rebounder with child on your lap and recite rhymes, count with the bounce as you bounce (your feet can be on floor, or if you can sit child in between your crossed legs and bounce with your own inertia).

PRESCHOOL / TODDLERS up to age 4

(Introduce new children by doing the previous Straddling and Sitting modes)

1. "HIT YOUR KNEE" -CROSS KNEE HIT :
(child lying with back on rebounder)

Bring child's Right hand to touch Left knee as you bend the Left leg so knee comes to chest, saying:

"Hit your knee, hit your knee, ONE, TWO, THREE.
Hit your knee, hit your knee, UNO, DOS, TRES."

Reverse, other leg & hand.

(Note: see the sneaky way to introduce bilingualism?-use child's native language for the second line)

2. "YELLOW, RED & GREEN LIGHT: PEDDLING MY BICYCLE"
(lying on back—ankles being held by one assisting)

"I'm riding on my bicycle, and pedaling real slow... slow....slow

('peddle' the child's legs by holding onto ankles. Point to yellow light

or colored circle on your pre-made 'stoplight')

And when I see the big green light I know it's time to go, go-go-go-go!

(pump the child's legs faster and faster after pointing to the green light

or have another child point to it)

I'm pedaling so fast and soon I say 'Oh no, no-no

Because I see a yellow light begin to glow, glow, glow

I slow right down just as the light turns red... red... red

And I then I STOP (clap feet together right on that word)

So I won't fall and bump my little head, head, head!

3. **"KNEES DROP NOW!"**

    (assist by holding hands of child and accenting the words rhythmically on the contact

    with the mat)

Jumping, Jumping, Jumping on the Rebounder

Jumping, Jumping, knee-drop NOW!

(child can determine how to fall, but later you can be specific and how the child

drop to knees, saying: " knee drop NOW!," working to have the contact of

knees to mat on <u>'NOW'</u>. This is where the coordination and brain/body link

gets developed)

Knees Drop Now!

Sheila Steele's
BOUNCING GROSS MOTOR LAB

OBJECTIVES:

- To prepare students for reading, assuring the Vestibular-Ocular reflex (VOR) is activated.
- To correct imbalances between brain and body to prevent falling, by sending messages to the appropriate muscles for contraction: Vestibular-Kinetic Reflex (VKR)
- To build self-confidence so that behavior doesn't have to be a problem
- To allow neural brain network to be stimulated and grow
- To develop ability to remember limited sequence of moves with ease in transition
- To develop auditory coordination (chants) with bounce moves.

NOTES: SUGGESTED PROTOCOL

1. I pre-tested for laterality: right or left dominance, and whether they could cross the midline with hitting opposite knee: I ask:

    > *"(a) Raise your Right hand. (b) Left foot. (c) Left hand.*
    > *(d) Right Foot. (e) Raise a knee and cross over with your*
    > *opposite arm, like this….Can you keep going with each knee*
    > *and opposite hand?"*

You will find this reveals who has learning problems, so that you can work with them! Recall my mentioning that 'laterality' was a prime indicator of learning ability

2. For the first six lessons, I taught only the first six moves until the children had it in memory what came next. (World, Tigger, Chicken, Teeter, Hippo, Knee Drop)

3. Then I added the educational component of the phonics program which I mentioned earlier (in the Lymphatic 'Choo-Choo' Breathing) where they intoned the letter sound on the down-bounce, rhythmically.

4. When I could see that this was easily facilitated, I re-tested for laterality. There was always some improvement because I preceded each session with the cross-knee warm-up.

5. Next, I added spelling of their name Forward, Backward, Forward (challenging the brain development with the backward spelling, but always finishing <u>forward</u> to reconnect the learning pattern). You might be amazed at how well they do!

6. Because I taught six to eight children at a time in a 'center' grouping, I had those waiting, sitting with shoes off, sitting in a line. (Note: shoes on is ok, but there is a greater benefit for 'electrical' stimulation if the feet are more directly in contact with the mat). The child whose turn it would be next, was holding a stuffed animal or pointer stick and acted as 'teacher' with me – saying what comes next. I had other stations where kids rotated and not idle.

Other centers might include:

balance beam
foot slammer
jumprope
beanbag toss

Demonstrations and ordering of these products are given during workshops. See end of manual.

7. All of this first segment is given a time allotment of 2-3 minutes per child during any session, to avoid restlessness. They performed 3 of the animal moves only, then sat to watch the others finish, focusing on saying the chants with the one rebounding.

8. Strict instruction and understanding of this routine is great training and self-discipline. A parent or classroom aide is suggested to monitor the movement from one activity to the next. I award points to the groups that are following the rules.

9. When the group could master 'World' through 'Knee Drop', I then introduced the remaining segment 'Kangaroo' through 'Thumper'. They will thoroughly enjoy the success and fun when they can do the whole routine (about 10 minutes per child) during individual assessment.

10. ADDING THE TIMES TABLES OR SIGHT WORD OR SPELLING TO THE REBOUNDING.

Do the math, sight or sound reading flash cards while bouncing, with words getting more difficult as mastery achieved. Remember to say the correct response on the bottom of the bounce.

Kanagroo Bounce

Moving to Learn
BOUNCING
Gross Motor Lab

Twisting Around the Small World

Tigger Tail Bounce

Chicken Bounce

Teeter-Totter Toes

Happy Hippopotamus

Knee Drop

Kangaroo Bounce

Jumping Jackrabbit

Cheetah Chase

Teeter-Totter Toes/ Tigger Tail (repeat for cool down)

Froggie Feet

Clam

Crab

Thumper

Try to do in stocking feet to trigger the 'electric' energy reflexes in the feet:

Warm-up with the cross-knee hit (opposite hand to knee)

1. **TWISTING AROUND THE "SMALL WORLD"**

   - Starting position: sitting on the rebounder, feet on floor.
   - Try to have derriere on the mat part
   - Use own inertia to bounce around one direction for first 2 lines of song, sing:

   It's a small world after all,

   it's a small world after all

   (option of now changing direction around mat)

   It's a small world after all, it's a small,

   small world

Final OBJECTIVE: Use arms in opposition to legs? Move in smooth rhythm?

---

2. **"TIGGER TAIL"** – sitting cross-legged on the rebounder, use own inertia to bounce on 'tail' .

   chant:

   Tiggers are wonderful things

   Their tops are made of rubber

   Their bottoms made out of springs

   Bouncy, Bouncy, Fun, Fun, Fun

   A Tigger's the Only One!

Final OBJECTIVE: Can use own inertia without hands on?

---

3. **"CHICKEN BOUNCE"** – gently bounce on knees using own inner inertia.
   (or, adults prefer to stand, twisting knees in/heels out at same time as elbows out, then reverse)

   Flap your elbows (back of hands bent under armpits) like chicken wings. Sing:

   Chick – Chick – Chick – Chicken

   Lay a little egg for me!

   (repeat)

Final OBJECTIVE: If standing: coordinate elbows & heels out while knees in?

4. **"TEETER-TOTTER TOES"** – alternate raising heel of one foot, pressing toes down; helps to 'pop' knees forward. Hands at waist. Create inertia to gentle bounce.

chant:

> *Teeter-Totter Toes*
> *(UH!—making sound, or do a clap)*
> *Teeter-Totter Toes (sound/clap)*
> *Teeter-Totter, Bread and Water*
> *Teeter-Totter Toes*

<u>Final OBJECTIVE</u>: understand the 'alternate' concept of shifting weight?

---

5. **"HAPPY HIPPO"** – begin by simply twisting both HEELS at the same time in one direction, without lifting TOES off mat. Twist in other direction by slightly lifting heels; keep up the pattern. When able, use fists to hit hips: twisting hips & heels to R, hitting hip with R hand (whichever hip is out, that gets hit.)

chant:

> *Happy Hippo-pot-amus,*
> *Happy Hippo-pot-amus*
> *Hap-hap-happy, Hip-hip-hippy*
> *Happy Hippo-pot-amus*

<u>Final OBJECTIVE</u>: twisting of feet back and forth with homolateral fist& hip

---

6. **"KNEES DROP NOW!"** – assist by holding hands of standing child to make sure they jump and drop on mat and not too close to edge. They get to enjoy a higher bounce now.

chant:

> *Jumping, Jumping, Jumping on the Rebounder*
> *Jumping, Jumping, Knees drop NOW...*
> *Knees drop NOW.....Knees drop NOW*
> (yes, do 3 knee drops)

<u>Final OBJECTIVE</u>: Dropping to knees on auditory cue 'Now'.

31

NOTE: **After completing the Knee-Drop, PROCEED to EXIT off rebound mat with a <u>SEAT DROP</u>** and stay down to slide off. Jumping off is discouraged for injuries and shock to joints.

Next is the continued set of exercises to be added on, or taught as a separate grouping for memorization.

7. "<u>**KANGAROO**</u>" – jumping tall; hands fisted at chest height. Rise off the mat with straight legs, extending arch of foot so that toes point down (this won't be easy, as they will want to bend knees as jump.)

chant:

Kangaroo, Kangaroo, Jump so high

Kangaroo, Kangaroo, Up to the sky! (3x)

<u>Final OBJECTIVE</u>: achieve some height? Able to point toes downward while in air? Keep legs straight? Hands fisted at chest?

---

8. "**JUMPING JACKRABBIT**" – as indicated, it is a jumping jack on the rebounder – coordination with open-close of legs to the bounce of the mat might take time. Thus, doing it on the floor FIRST, is suggested to practice the jumping jack movement. I start off by saying, "Open, Close, Open, Close, Open, Close, ½ turn". That way they get the idea of arm-leg movement.

chant:

Jumping Jack,   *Jumping Jack,*
(open)   (close)   *(open)   (close)*

Jumping Jack   *RAB - BIT*
(open)   (close)   *(do 2 ordinary jumps while ½ turn, with two claps)*

<u>Final OBJECTIVE</u>: arms, legs moving out together? Closing arms/legs at same time?

---

9. "<u>**CHEETAH CHASE**</u>" – running fast on spot, in time with the bounce rhythm.

chant:

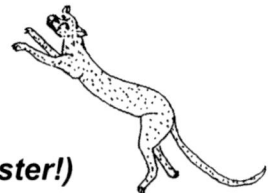

Cheetah, Cheetah, run, run, run

Cheetah, Cheetah, having fun (repeat , faster!)

<u>Final OBJECTIVE</u>: Can coordinate words with bounce, alternating feet and increasing pace?

Note: optional, but suggested to try for smooth transition from Cheetah to the next set: REPEAT THE "**TEETER-TOTTER TOES**" AND "**TIGGER TAIL**" prior to COOL-DOWN

10. "**FROGGIE FEET**" – sit on floor, with feet raised onto rebounder. Massage gait points, outside and between toes (remember this can also be taught to children to do while sitting and waiting turns.)

    sing:

    > *One Little, Two Little, Three Little Tadpoles*
    > *Four Little, Five Little, Six Little Tadpoles,*
    > *Seven Little, Eight Little, Nine Little Tadpoles,*
    > *Ten Tadpole FROGGIE Feet.*

    (an educational point: teach that tadpoles are baby frogs)

    <u>Final OBJECTIVE</u>: Children imagine they are thanking their feet for doing such a good job, by massaging feet; that that actually helps their brain work better!

---

11. "**CLAM**" – Abdominals, lying on back, on floor, knees bent and feet on rebounder. Do abdominal crunches, raising head and torso to thighs, doing lymphatic 'choo-choo' breathing (sh, sh, sh-sh-sh) while coming up, and inhale as return to floor; opening and closing torso, like clam shell.

    <u>Final OBJECTIVE</u>: Able to raise torso from floor while keeping feet on rebounder mat?

---

12. "**CRAB**" – Backward push-up (triceps): sitting on floor with arms behind and hands on the rebounder, push body up as straighten arms (exhale at the same time) and return to sitting. Body up as straighten arms (exhale at same time), and return to sitting.

    <u>Final OBJECTIVE</u>: Can use strength in arms to carry weight?

---

13. "**THUMPER**" – Standing, thump your thyroid (just below collar bones and clavicles) – to stimulate metabolism. Thyroid hormone affects almost all body cells; regulates tissue growth, skeleton and nerves.

    <u>Final OBJECTIVE</u>: Understand that tapping thyroid area wakes up body? (adults: stimulates metabolism)

Moving to Learn –

ADDITIONAL GROSS MOTOR - REBOUNDING

1. COUNTING by 2's, by 5's, and 10's, as high as child can go. Record in the 'pre' column the highest number attained and record date. **Make sure the counting is accented on the contact with the mat**. Each number should take TWO bounces, that is, a bounce between each vocal count.

2. 'SEE & SAY' VISION COORDINATION: Hold up word cards for child to focus and say. Such as: rhyming sequence "dog, log, fog"; or sound out each letter on the bounce, then say the word three times on the bounce. The flash cards should have lettering large enough for student to read and focus (one –two inches). Stand no further than four feet away to begin with. Take note if you have to move in closer or further away for child to see the letters clearly.

3. LIFT ONE KNEE OFF MAT – 8 counts, change legs. See if child can add the opposite hand to knee.

4. COPY CAT ARM SEQUENCE – see separate chart; coordinate with bounce.

HIGHER OBJECTIVES OF THIS ADDITIONAL LAB:

- To prepare students for reading, assuring the Vestibular-Ocular Reflex (VOR) is activate.

- To help correct imbalances between brain and body to prevent falling, by sending messages to the appropriate muscles for contraction – the Vestibular-Kinetic Reflex (VKR).

Froggie Feet

The Crab

Twisting Around the Small World

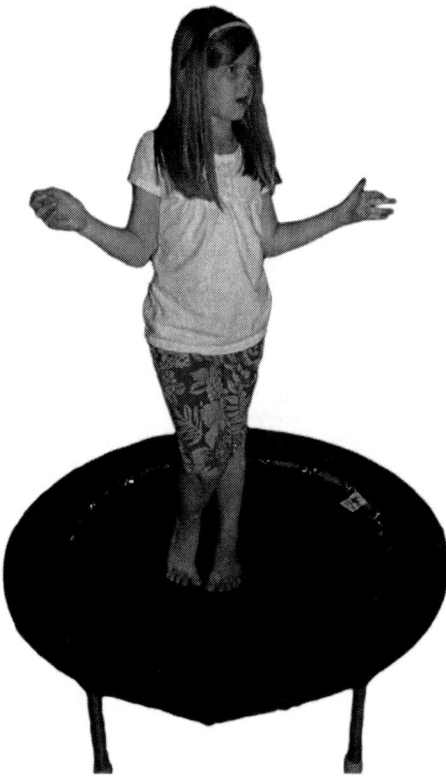

Teeter-Totter Toes

Kangaroo Bounce

Cheetah Chase

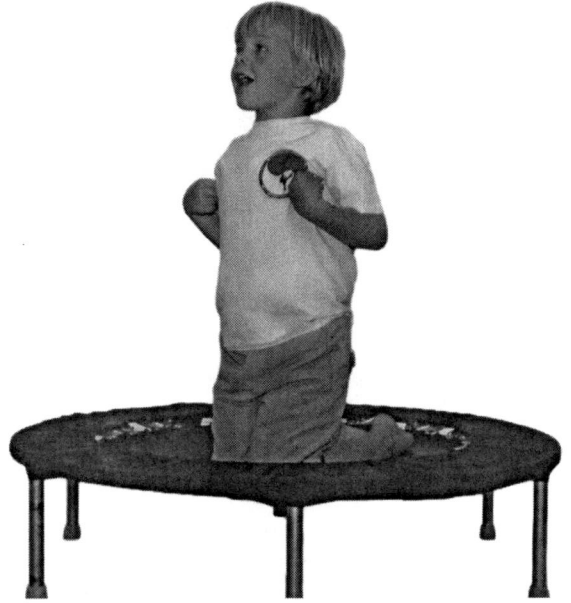
Chicken Bounce

Twisting Around the Small World

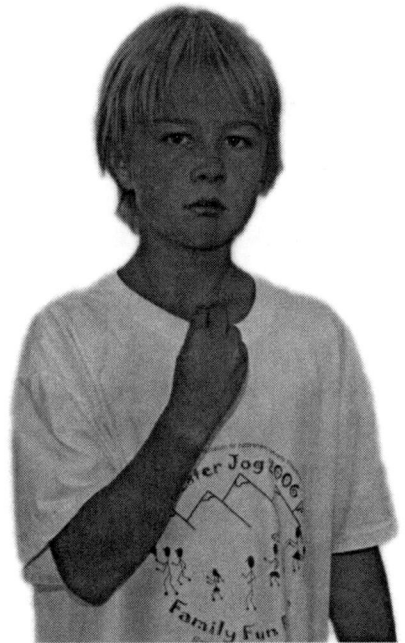
Thumper

Tigger Tail Bounce

Tigger Tail Bounce

Happy Hippo

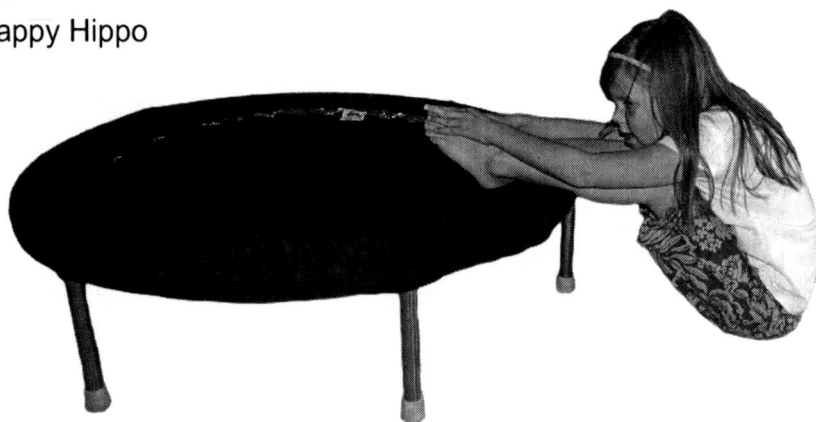

Clam

EVALUATION : GROSS MOTOR BOUNCING LAB (animal moves)

In all cases, a verbal chant is assigned to be coordinated with the bouncing (see notes) CHECKMARK if successful in PRETEST column during first two days, record date. 'MINUS' SIGN if needs improvement ,POST results after 30 days or end of term

NAME	AROUND THE WORLD sit and twist in both directions while bouncing and singing?		TIGGER TAIL & CHICKEN Uses own inertia for BOTH; bounce from seated or kneeling position		TEETER TOES Change weight with each bounce?		HAPPY HIPPO Both feet twist heels same side as hip being hit?		KANGAROO When airborne, are arches of feet Stretched (toes downward)?		CHEETAH Able to lift knees alternately,, and keep timing of chant with each contact on mat?	
	PRE	POST	PRE	POST	PRE	POST	PRE	POST	PRE	POST	PRE	POST
1												
2												
3												
4												
5												
6												
7												
8												
9												
10												
11												
12												

Copy Cat Arm Chart

Follow the diagram on the next page from L. to R., changing each pose on the 'bounce'. Repeat. [Tape Chart to Wall]

This CopyCat Chart is a series of arm movements to be executed **on** the bounce. The important use of this is to secure the VOR (see below). Otherwise, words dance around on the page and readers lose their place. The part of our neural network responsible for balance is the Vestibular system:

VESTIBULAR SYSTEM: ORGANS RESPONSIBLE FOR GIVING US FEEDBACK ABOUT BALANCE. Three semi-circular canals located in the inner ear are like inner gyroscopes. Information from these organs is processed in clusters of brain cells deep in the brain stem, where information received from the senses is **integrated**.

We possess two Vestibular Reflexes:
Vestibulo-Kinetic Reflex (VKR)
Vestibulo-Ocular Reflex (VOR)

VKR: Helps us correct imbalances when falling by sending messages to the muscles needed to contract.

VOR: allows us to fix our eyes on an object while the rest of our body is moving (as on the mini-trampoline). Without this important reflex working properly, the precise eye movement required for reading will not be possible.

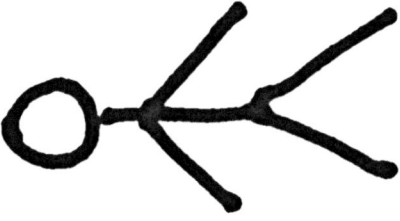

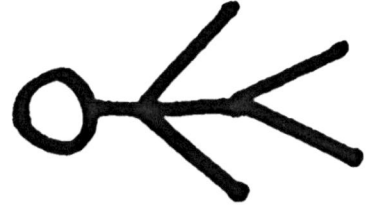

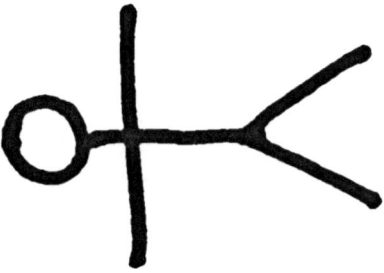

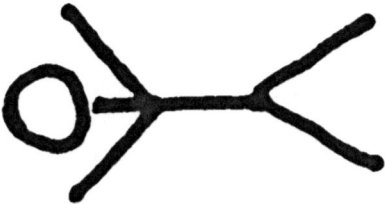

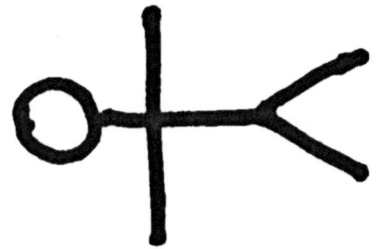

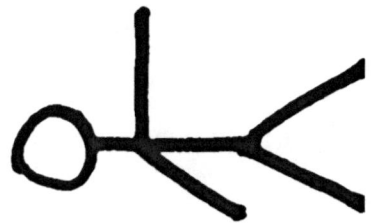

To purchase quality NEEDAK REBOUNDER:

You receive a discount by contacting and ordering through author, Sheila Steele, but by all means check out the NEEDAKMFG.COM website for product details. There are imitators, so be sure you get to the 'home' company.

Want a Workshop in your area?

Sheila has given workshop demonstrations and trainings in Canada, U.S. and South Africa. The BALANCE & BOUNCE workshop includes use of a balance board as part of the training, and another manual "Coming to Your Senses." For your workshop requests, contact publisher, or Sheila directly by email: sheilasteele@ymail.com. The next page has a sample workshop flyer for you to recruit interested parties for direct instruction by Sheila.

Note that the following resources were credited in the text of the manual, and that the *Animal Moves Chart was author's original creation while working in South Africa, 1997*.

CREDITS

Carter, Albert E., Miracles of Rebound Exercise, 1979

Gettman, Dr. G.N., O.D., in "Miracles of Rebound Exercise" and report on "Learning Connections Program in Queensland Schools) Sept. 2000

Haebig, Jeff, Ph.D.: exploring the neuroscience of learning via website Wellnessquest.com, 2006

West, Samuel, The Golden Seven Plus One – Conquer Disease, Samuel Publishing Co., UT, 1981

NEEDAKMFG.COM

BALANCE & BOUNCE LAB
To improve Academics, Health and Behavior

Contact Person:
Location:
Time:

Training Workshop for:	Trainer: Sheila Steele B.Ed, SOI, CL/R

Training Workshop for:

- Daycare/Preschool
- Counselors
- School teachers
- Occupational Therapists
- Vocational Schools
- Elderly
- Concerned Parents
- Penal Institutions
- Tutors
- Brain Injured
- Seekers of Knowledge

Trainer: Sheila Steele B.Ed, SOI, CL/R
With 20 years professional experience and enthusiasm, has taught in Canada, South Africa and the U.S.

People say:
"It's the most practical workshop I have ever had, with real application"
I'm amazed. My pre-school kids settle down after the balance board"
"Using the rebounder, I definitely don't get as sick as I used to."

Balance & Bounce Lab was designed by Sheila Steele. The 'BALANCE" uses a balance board, the 'BOUNCE" uses the mini-trampoline (rebounder), with visual, auditory and kinesthetic activities to relieve stress and prepare for learning. In clinical studies, it has been proven that children or adults who have learning or behavior problems are not 'sensorily integrated' – they do not have a comfort level of movement in space, usually cannot read well, and suffer anxiety. IT'S TIME TO APPLY THESE NON-INVASIVE TECHNIQUES FOR INDIVIDUAL AND COMMUNITY WELL-BEING!

This 4-hour workshop will certify you as having been trained in the application of safe and fun activities. Address is above. Fee is _____, and includes manual "Learning to Move - BOUNCING Gross Motor Lab"

Pre-registation required by _____
Space is Limited

Note to organizers: A minimum of 6 people required for a workshop; Trainer's airfare and hotel must be included in the price of workshop, split among the participants.

This page intentionally left blank.

3936288